TIE
THE
KNOT

THAI THE KNOT

*How to Untangle the Complexities
of Cross-cultural Marriage*

Pop Soisangwan

BLACKSMITH BOOKS

Thai the Knot

ISBN 978-988-19002-6-5

Published by Blacksmith Books
5th Floor, 24 Hollywood Road, Central, Hong Kong
Tel: (+852) 2877 7899
www.blacksmithbooks.com

Illustrations by Ming

Contents

Introduction

After a whirlwind romance or by a matchmaker's luck, you've decided to devote your life, and any money that you might make from now until your death, to a Thai woman. I don't mean a one-night stand or a casual romp with the same woman during your annual hedonistic venture to the Land of Smiles; I'm speaking of holy matrimony, or something like it. A long-term commitment… a deeper understanding… a joining of hands, putting the plough into the soil… basically I mean the hardest work God created for man: marriage.

When you tell your friends and family members that you have fallen in love with a Thai woman and want to father her children, you may hear one or both of the following responses: "That's great!" or "Are you out of your mind?" The response depends on how that person feels toward marriage, and how they feel about cross-cultural marriage in general. Any news of marriage is wonderful news because most people believe that marriage is a beautiful thing, whether it is with someone who speaks the same language or not. However, don't be surprised if your announcement is met with an attempt to talk you out of the difficulties you will face when marrying a "foreigner."

So what are these difficulties that result in marrying a foreign woman? For many this means a language barrier or social difficulties, such as dealing with the stares in restaurants, the comments about your mixed children, and curiosity about what language you use together. For others, it means the small things that pop up every day, too numerous to list and hardly definable with just one example.

In this book, I'll illustrate the small things; small today, big tomorrow. This book is help for the helpless and hapless, a guide to help you navigate the shark-infested waters (read: annoying habits that make you want to shove your foot up your spouse's behind) of a committed relationship with a Thai.

The topics you'll find in this book have not been discussed in published form before, at least not in contexts that you'll read about. There are plenty of books in bookstores across Thailand that can teach you the ins-and-outs of how not to offend the Thais, how to do business with the Thais, how to *wai*, how to bargain with street vendors and not point with your feet. The last thing I want to do is sound like a broken record because my husband calls me a broken record every time we fight… and though I have yet to figure out what this means, I know broken records can't sound good. So I'm not going to rehash what has been written and republished every year. Instead, I want to discuss the subtleties of how to live with someone who grew up in a land far, far away, speaking a peculiar language.

Let me reiterate that this book is not for Westerners looking for a one night stand or a temporary arrangement with a long-haired sleeping dictionary. Dating couples could use this book, but only if they plan on living together long-term. The man who has his girlfriend stay with him one or two nights a week will not have experienced some of the pitfalls of relationships that I will mention here; however, don't let that stop you from spending money on this book.

So how is this book organized and how should you use it? Easy, start at page one and read until the end. The topics are not necessarily arranged in chronological order. Issues that come up during the dating period may appear later in the book, while topics on marriage may appear anywhere. At the beginning, I will discuss incidents that can occur in the first year of marriage – in other words, the shocking eye-openers. Hopefully you, the Westerner, will use my advice and implement it when building your relationship with your Thai mate. As most cross-cultural relationships stereotyped in Thai media indicate a Western male/Thai female combination, I write mostly for that angle; however, there is no reason why the opposite gender counterparts or males from other parts of the world should not benefit from this book too.

If your Thai spouse has good English-language skills, I hope you sit or lie down and read together. You may find yourselves within these pages. If not, and you end up reading alone, then don't worry – your Thai spouse will notice and appreciate the changes as you try harder to increase the understanding and harmony between you.

Enjoy!

Pop Soisangwan

What is a Thai woman?

A Thai point of view is as relevant as any other

1

Are women of different skin different?

My dear husband told me of a conversation he'd had with a friend. My husband informed this friend that he was culturally prepared to marry an Asian woman. He bragged of his open-mindedness and ability to handle the difficulties that would come with a cross-cultural marriage. His friend listened patiently, and then responded with something simple but profound. He said, "A woman's a woman. It doesn't matter where she's from." My husband described to me how that statement bowled him over. His eyes were opened and he saw the truth, and it set him free.

Maybe there's no extra layer of hardship within a cross-cultural relationship. A man has to learn to live with a female, whether she's Thai or Western, rich or poor, dark-skinned or fair-skinned, an honored scholar or a country bumpkin who raises chickens. All women are equally challenging, each with a unique personality, matchless quirks, and exceptional demands. Man cannot undo what God has done, so he just has to learn to live with her.

Though I believe a cross-cultural relationship does involve some extra level of struggle, I do agree with the point that women's basic needs are universal. Our needs surpass religion, politics, language, culture, and social status. Gentlemen, we want your attention. We want your time. We want you to cuddle us. We want to be number one in your hearts. And we want gold, diamonds, and cash (there's the hard truth!). If you can discover and understand what your woman's needs are, then you are well on your way to a successful relationship. But, knowing her needs is not enough; you'll have to meet them!

So how can you discover her needs? It's easy – read the preceding paragraph again. The keys are there. *Attention, Time, Affection,* and

Support. Whether your wife is from Bangkok, Songkhla, Chiang Rai or Nongkai, she has a void in her life, and she needs those four things to make her feel secure and loved. Must I go through each key and define them? If you're reading this book, then that means you are truly interested in knowing how to prepare yourself to take care of your Thai spouse, so go through them I will.

Attention doesn't mean looking at her or throwing her a glance once in a while. It means putting down the newspaper while she's talking with you. It means pressing pause on the DVD player when she comes into the room and has something to say. It means not letting your eyes wander when another dark, honey-skinned beauty walks by. Focus on her, and she'll be happy.

My former boss spoke at my wedding reception, and this was his advice for my husband: a Thai woman is like a cat. Rub her the right way, and she'll be content. Stroke her the wrong way, and her claws will come out. It's so true! But, again, I think this could be true for women around the world. Giving her your attention is petting her the right way, not irritating her fur.

Time is closely related to attention. It's a sign of devotion. It's comforting for a woman to know that the man will be there when she needs him. If she works late and calls to ask if you could escort her home because it's so dark outside, will you do it? If yes, give yourself a point for Time. If not, you'd better start searching for a way to apologize, if she indeed makes it home safely.

Perhaps your wife feels an obligation to help a friend in need, and she tries to enlist your help. If you say, "But that's your friend's job," then you are back to square one in trying to understand her. However, if you help her fulfill her promise to a friend, then give yourself another point for Time. I've promised friends that I'd check their written English and then I asked my husband, a native English speaker, for help. For him, it was a great sacrifice of his own time to help someone he hadn't met. He hadn't promised to check my friend's English – I had. But for a Thai woman, when she responds to a friend's plea, that plea, in her eyes, becomes a plea to her husband too. Sacrifice your time for your wives, men. The 'you-scratch-my back, I-scratch-your-back' mentality is very strong in Thailand. If you help her, you can ask for some of her "time" in bed. She can't refuse your requests because now she owes you!

And this leads to the third key: **Affection**. For a woman, this could mean a sniff of her neck (we'll get to sniffing in Thai culture later on) or a touch of the hand. For men, rough and dirty sex. With such a wide range of acts of affection, it's a wonder that men and women can live together.

So what displays of affection does a Thai girl respond best to? Well, in public, forget it. A Thai girl doesn't need you to paw all over her in a shopping mall. It's considered low class (and class is another thing we'll come to later) to act like a Western couple in public. Kissing on the lips and grabbing her ass is not how to show it, either. You will embarrass her in front of others. And no, her smile does not mean that she approves! Remember, we're talking about the kind of woman you would marry, not a bar girl for a quickie. (If a bar girl *is* the one you want to marry, then heaven help you). That type of girl is used to having someone's hands all over her in public, so why not yours? Most of them have resolved that issue, emotionally separating themselves from certain Thai cultural norms.

So what can you do? You can hold her hand, touch her elbow when she walks a flight of stairs, stay close when going up and down the escalator, or carry her bags or open doors for her.

You might say, "Wait! I don't see Thai men doing those things!" Yes, it may sound old-fashioned to many Westerners, but you can quickly become the popular and gossiped-over stud in Thailand if you begin to do those things for your sweetheart. Affection is something many Thai men are unable to show. Statistics may demonstrate the decline of marriage and the prevalence of divorce in the West, but just because a Thai couple doesn't divorce, it doesn't mean that the marriage is a happy one. Marriage in Thailand is still, in many cases, an economic contract. A man needs offspring to carry on his name, take care of him in old age and cook and clean for him. A woman needs someone to take care of her and her parents financially. But many Thai wives do wish for a more affectionate husband. Thai women would climb over each other for a man who is affectionate to her and willing to fulfill her basic needs.

Trust me and try it. Your woman will be the envy of all others because she won't be able to keep the secret that her husband is affectionate, not leaving out one sultry detail.

When you two are alone, there are hardly any rules on affection. Unless she has some serious hang-ups or issues, she understands that her body belongs to you. We'll talk about that in a later chapter too, but just treat her with respect in public and she'll let go of most inhibitions with you in the bedroom.

P'Tum of Bangkok has been married for seven years to a British man. Her advice to men seeking a Thai soulmate is to understand that Thai women appreciate the man taking on several roles in the relationship. Her husband is her lover, friend, father, and son. She takes care of him as though he were a child, yet loves him to dote on her like a father.

Support is the last key. This is where I disagree with my husband and his colleague. There *are* exceptions between women of different cultures.

Western men may moan about how Thai women and their families just want their money, and this is a difficult issue for many cross-cultural couples to resolve. But I believe I can help explain the concept of Support. In Thailand, many women do not have the privileges or opportunities to earn the (relatively) high salaries that Western women can. Things are changing, but change is slow. Also, remember that Thailand doesn't have a social security system and lacks the economic safety nets that other countries have. For most Thais, when you're sick, you don't work. If you don't work, you don't bring in a salary. Workers' compensation may be available in foreign companies and some Thai businesses, but for the masses, there's no such thing.

Perhaps Thais are expected to take care of their families because there's no choice or alternative. Thais think Westerners are heartless because they don't 'take care' of their parents (here, 'taking care' means letting your parents live with you until they die, and pampering them by doing things that they are certainly capable of doing for themselves, in addition to giving them money every month). Well, give Thailand strong retirement, investment, and social security programs, and I'm sure

Thailand would start to look like the United States, Australia, or some other Western country. Older couples would be financially independent and buy retirement homes in Hua Hin or Cha-am where they'd be far away from their children. Sometimes cultural values are a result of financial necessities, not of some absolutes or universal truth.

Anyway, I say this to explain that Thai women aren't greedy vampires looking for dollars or pounds to suck out of you. You are expected, since you have the 'privilege' and 'opportunity' of making a good salary, to help support her financially and, yes, depending on the social status of your wife's family, her parents too. I haven't mentioned the differences in social classes, but it's important to state here that the lower your wife's social status is, the more you're going to be paying through your wallet. The higher she is, the more independent she'll be, and the lesser burden she and her parents will be upon you.

It's a norm in Thailand for the most privileged individual to treat the less fortunate; or the one of higher status to take care of the one of lower. For example, when a group of Thai office managers have lunch together, the manager with the highest rank, which usually means the highest salary, will be expected to pay the bill. So if your wife's parents do not have much money coming in each month, and you do, they are not greedy, they are just following the norm. You can accept it or go marry a blonde.

I don't mean to be harsh, but you'll be much happier with your Thai wife if you don't fight things and learn to accept them. Those who have lived in Thailand for any meaningful length of time have learned that the more you fight to make things work in Thailand, the more they don't work.

So to sum up, a Thai woman's basic needs are not really different from the needs of women of any other country. Focus your eyes on her, sacrifice your time, show affection properly, and make them feel financially secure. And where there's a layer of cultural norms which seem to affect her needs, the following chapters will explain what your response should be.

2

The different types of Thai women

It's easy to pigeonhole a nationality or ethnic group. I sometimes catch myself saying "Americans are like this…" or "Americans don't like to do that…", but the Americans I'm referring to may just be two or three people I have observed. So if you are under the impression that all Thai women are sweet and committed to their husbands, then you may be setting yourself up for a big disappointment. Not all Thai women are the same. Not all are sweet, innocent, submissive or committed to romantic relationships. Some are out to get you – or get what's in your bank account – and leave you high and dry.

When a Thai speaks, other Thais can accurately guess the speaker's level of education and social status. Speech reveals more than a regional accent. This is true with almost any language. For instance, people from the northeast part of Thailand, Isaan, are the butt of many Thai jokes because of the region's 'backwardness.' Isaan has its own dialect, closer to the Lao language than Thai, with quirky vocabulary and pronunciation. Most Thais know at least a few Isaan words and will use them in their conversations if they want to tease someone for a thoughtless act. In Thai, we also have a saying: "Don't be so Lao." This means, don't be ignorant. And since Isaan is closely associated with Lao culture, the two words are often synonymous. The point is that the dialect carries a meaning, often a negative one.

But what if a Thai meets a woman from Isaan who holds a master's degree and is a working professional? Will she lose her accent? Not entirely. A Thai will hear the accent and know she came from Isaan, no matter how she tries to hide it by using the Bangkok dialect. But will the Thai hear the speech of a backward Isaan person or hear the diction of a professional woman? They will notice that our fictitious woman is educated and professional, despite the fact that she may have a slight regional dialect in her spoken Thai. Differences in Thai women are deeper than regional accents. Their speech reveals so much more.

However, many foreign men are not aware that these differences exist, or they do not understand that they need to be aware of the class of the woman they wish to marry. There are many educated, professional men who come to Thailand and fall in love with Thai women, unwittingly strutting around Bangkok with country bumpkins speaking Thai as if their language stopped developing after the sixth grade, with the social graces to match. Fortunately many of these women, who deserve love as much as anyone else, find the foreign men that deserve them.

I've been to formal company parties where the president or managing director, a foreign man, brought his wife for everyone to meet. Sadly, no one felt comfortable conversing with this wife. Despite the husband's 200,000 baht monthly salary, it was spent on dressing her up when it could have been better spent sending her to finishing school.

I have to bring this up, not because I look down on my fellow Thai women, but because there are many wonderful, educated women wondering why all the ones of lower class get the nice foreign men! I'm not recommending that you chase after the snootiest, most arrogant, Gucci-bag toting Thai woman, but even they can be conquered by a charming foreigner if you choose to be patient and not be intimidated… and if you feel that the plastic you find after you peel away the brand-name clothes is worth it! No, there is a large group of females stuck in the middle, who for various reasons don't get the opportunity to be romanced by sincere foreign men.

There's a word in the Thai vocabulary that is a corruption of an English word. It is *spec*. It comes from the word 'specifications.' In Thai, the word *spec* means the physical characteristics of the type of person that you fancy. Have you noticed that Thai and Western men never fight over the same woman? That's because they have different specs. Let me describe the Thai man's spec for his ideal woman. She is tall, has white skin, full cheekbones with a sharp nose, usually obtained after surgery, and big round eyes, also achieved by the surgeon's knife. Look at many of the local fashion magazines and you'll see the typical Thai spec. The most important part is the white skin. Thai girls strive to be white. There are whitening creams filling shelf after shelf in the supermarkets. One brand is for her face, another for her arms and legs, and yet another for her armpits. Dark-complexioned skin is thought of as dirty. It is the skin tone of the working class, the farmers, and all those funny-sounding people from Isaan. Yuck!

The Western man's spec is very different. These girls are dark, very dark, and flat-faced with wide noses and smaller eyes. From a Thai person's point of view, the difference is almost comical. This is why Thai men do not feel threatened by Western men. Westerners chase after the 'leftovers.'

Let me give you this analogy. For readers familiar with American culture, or lack of it, imagine good-looking, educated, financially stable Asian men, with stirrings in their loins, coming to the hollows of West Virginia to court trailer trash. Or picture the character Ting Tong

Macadangdang from the television series *Little Britain*, one of my favorite shows. That is what Thais see as the typical Thai wife of a Westerner. You may argue that even the least educated and socially underdeveloped Thai girl is heads above any trailer trash from the States or any character that Matt Lucas can come up with, and I may even agree with you, but from the Thai point of view this is how it looks. A Thai point of view is as relevant as any other, so who is to say it is wrong?

Why is it so easy for ignorant Westerners to come to Thailand and quickly hook up with someone? The answer makes sense. The middle and upper class girls are more reserved and conservative. You have to take your time with them. The ones at the lower end are willing to make the first move or, if you make the first move, they won't put up any barriers. Their pickings are slim, and many hold the notion that all foreigners are rich. They can also be found working in the industries closest to tourism, thus putting them in close proximity to Western men.

So be careful. If you have a girlfriend within the first month of being in Thailand, then congratulations, you may have found the West Virginian equivalent. (Actually, my husband told me to use West Virginia as an example. He wouldn't let me use his home state).

So what is a Western man to do when he arrives in Thailand? He shouldn't stay holed up in his apartment. How can he spot the differences between Thai women when he goes out and begins meeting people? Well, there's nothing I can do or say to make the white-skinned Thai girls more appealing to the man who comes from a culture where they worship the sun when at the beach and lay in coffin-like contraptions to darken their skin. If the Western spec describes the type of woman you'd like to be with, then at least learn how to choose the one who is best for you. I recommend copying the checklist below and when you start meeting potential long-term mates, use the checklist to weed them out. If you follow my advice, you'll be doing a lot of weeding.

To make your burden light, try marrying as high up the social ladder as possible. Don't worry about marrying someone out of your league. It's difficult to marry above you, as Thai girls are not really open to marrying a man who is below them. But marrying far below you will create many headaches.

So how do we discern the differences between Thai women? The very first criterion is her language skill. How much English does she know? Yes, I know you want to learn to speak Thai, but the more English she knows, the better chance you have of communicating with each other, and better the chance that she will be able to tap into your culture and understand it.

You can still learn the Thai language while married to an English-speaking Thai woman. Be wary of the one who hasn't mastered a sentence of English, or does not understand that stress in English does NOT take place on the last syllable of every word. Does she still say *cenTRAN* for central? *SinGAN* for single? And everyone's favorite example: *kumpooDAA* for computer? If the answer is yes, she still has a long way to go to master English. You may find her *Tinglish* accent endearing, but try socializing with other Thais or Western expatriates and be forewarned they may roll their eyes at your ditzy-sounding date.

After you have found someone with adequate English-language skills (only you know how much skill you need her to have), then the next point to consider when determining her place on the social ladder is her educational background. Does she have a four-year degree? I think a two-year vocational degree should be the minimum. The more education she has obtained, the more discussions you'll be able to have together that don't only involve her admiration of your lovemaking techniques. If she has a science degree in such fields as Biology, Chemistry, or Computer Science, you can be a little lax on her language skills. Anyone interested in the sciences should be a well-rounded person anyway and doesn't need the English language skills to show it.

Are degrees from all institutions the same? No, not really. Here's the pecking order:

The government institutions usually take the brightest students. If she has a degree from Chulalongkorn, Thammasat, Chiang Mai, Khon Khaen, or Kasertsart, then she had the grades and accolades to get into Thailand's best institutions. I'd avoid girls who studied at private universities. Why? Because that could mean that they failed the university entrance exam, but their families were rich enough to send them to a private institution. They barely passed their program's degree requirements because there was little motivation to study hard due to a guaranteed job waiting for them in the family business. So they are both stupid and spoiled. Am I being too harsh again? I don't mean to say all students who attend private universities are rich and lazy, but it wouldn't hurt to raise a little red flag in your mind if you happen to become interested in a student or graduate of one such university.

Choosing a Thai woman who obtained a degree from abroad may not be the best choice either. Her English will be quite good but some of the students return to Thailand with a slanted view of the West. My husband, who is a lecturer at a university in the States, told me that less than 15 percent of international students in America ever get to visit an American home. I would hope that universities in other countries would have better programs for international students or more people who are interested in meeting these lonely students. Sadly, these students most likely lived on campus where they saw all kinds of debauchery. They probably never developed a relationship with a local family, never got to learn about the culture or the people, and hung out with other Thais and Asians while resenting their relegation to the outer fringes of the host country's society during their stay. So if you are interested in a Thai woman who spent a few years on a college campus abroad, ask her opinions of mainstream society in that country and be aware if all she says are negative generalizations. Remember, the odds are that she was not part of the 15 percent that was lucky enough to be invited inside a home to share a meal with a local family.

You need to strike a balance between the appropriate level of education and her down-to-earth attitude, and considering her institution of study is a good way to try to measure how balanced she is.

Here's the reason my husband chose to court me. It was because I had some knowledge that no other Thai girl he knew had. We were communicating through e-mail about a subject in Linguistics (I was taking a course in Linguistics at Chiang Mai University and had his card. He gave it to me in passing several months before. I remembered him saying that his degree was in Linguistics, so I contacted him with questions). Anyway, he told me that his mother's side of the family had some Native American ancestry and mentioned his tribe. I said, "Oh, I know of them," and I told him what I knew of their history, because I had read about them in an American Literature course. Well, at that moment, according to him, he fell in love with me – just because I demonstrated that I knew about more than my own culture and was interested in learning what was outside Thailand. I was very Thai, and still am. I consider myself a traditional Thai girl who is not ignorant of other cultures. So if you can find a girl with an interest in what lies beyond her world, then you may have found an interesting one.

The next way to test the smarts of your potential mate is to see how she dresses herself. And this again is for those who can't help but salivate for the honey-skinned Thai beauties and will forever avoid the white-skinned Thai girls. If she has dark skin and insists on wearing bright red, pink, or yellow clothes, run for it. Those colors should never be worn with dark skin. Sorry, but as an avid reader of fashion magazines, I can never accept it. A dark-skinned girl who is aware of her own body (another test of her intelligence and education) will know that she is, unfortunately, limited in the colors she can wear. She should stick to dark colors (black, brown), any shade of white and gray, and all earth tones. No neon, no pastels. I'm not a certified anthropologist, but if any research was done into the backgrounds of dark-skinned girls who wore pink and those who didn't, I would almost bet that there would be some glaringly obvious patterns with the girl's educational background, social status of her family, and maybe even her own IQ. This may not be true in Western culture, but it is in Thai culture, and now I'm passing this knowledge on to you.

The next thing to consider is her family. Try to get an idea of her father's (and her mother's) work. Does he work in a company? What position? Is he a policeman? What rank? Is he a taxi driver? Actually that might be just fine. Does he drive a tuk-tuk? Well, like I said before, if you marry a girl of lower status, you'll be marrying her parents too and

will have to pay to bring them *up* to your status. So if you are okay with that, then guess what, you've just won yourself free tuk-tuk rides around Bangkok.

A middle class income in Bangkok should begin at 20,000 baht per month. If her father makes that much and her mother works too, or does something to supplement the family income, then her parents shouldn't be so needy after you get married. Personally, I would aim for a father-in-law who makes at least 30,000 baht per month. But anything below 20K and the supplementing will come from you.

To sum up, finding a girl whose parents make as much or more than you do will certainly relieve the pressure on you to help.

Thai perceptions

The Thai woman will always escalate what you didn't intend to start, then justify her anger by believing you started it.

3

What do Thais think of you?

Since I've given you some clues on how to be judgmental and mercilessly critical of Thai women, and how to determine their social status, it is only fair that I also discuss you, the Westerner, and warn you of the stereotypes Thais have of you.

What is the Thai stereotype of a Westerner? Here are the most common descriptions: temperamental, paranoid, distant from his/her family, and stingy. From a Thai viewpoint, these labels are justified. But for many Westerners, they are victims of cultural misunderstandings. You should try your best to avoid having one of these labels attached to you.

Temperamental

In Thai, the word is *jai lorn* or hot-hearted. Think of it as 'hot-headed' in English. Raising your voice, regardless of the situation or your emotions, is a big no-no. You will make the Thais around you uncomfortable; maybe even reduce some to tears. For many, they'll harbor negative feelings about you forever (or until they learn to better understand Western culture, which they may not want to any more). You may probably wonder why raising your voice is so bad, even if you are telling an exciting story. But it is true; especially if you are just telling a story, don't raise your voice!

Here's a typical scenario many Westerners find themselves in. A man comes home to his Thai partner after having a rough day at work. He wants to share with his wife how a person at the office pissed him off that day. He proceeds to tell the story as he experienced it, with all the drama. He raises his voice, he flings his arms, and he boldly proclaims his disdain for that person at the office. A Western woman might say to her husband, in the most supportive way, "Wow, that person IS a total bitch! I don't blame you for being angry!" But the Thai will have a completely

different response. She will either give you the silent treatment, throw something at you, throw many things at you, run away while throwing things over her shoulder hoping at least one thing will hit you square in the face, or cry uncontrollably and ask why you are angry with her.

Meanwhile the Western man is left standing there wondering how the conversation suddenly became about his wife. He says, "No, honey, I was talking about someone at work." And he says her name again. But his Thai 'honey' is not satisfied. She still thinks he is angry with her. She won't stop crying or hitting him out of anger. Suddenly, he *does* become angry and the whole thing escalates even more.

So what happened? The Thai woman paid more attention to the style of the man's delivery than what was being said (for those of you who have noticed how Thais focus so much on the surface and appearance and not substance, this should make perfect sense). The man feels even more frustrated because he thought he would score points for 'sharing' his feelings, and rightfully so. But as soon as the volume increases, the Thai woman blocks out the meaning and interprets the raised voice as an attack against her. This situation happens wherever and whenever there is an opportunity for cross-cultural misunderstandings: in offices, restaurants, 7-11s, and taxis, between males and females, males and males, and females and females. It doesn't matter. Keep the volume of your voice down, no matter how exciting your story is.

There are other ways of showing yourself as someone who is '*jai lorn*': Rolling your eyes, sighing, dropping things on your desk or table, or any type of body language or noise that shows you have run out of patience. These actions will always work against you, especially in a marriage. The Thai woman will always escalate what you didn't intend to start, and then justify her anger by believing you started it.

Paranoid

This is another adjective Thais use to describe Westerners. In the West, there's an axiom: don't sign anything you don't understand. Well, here in Thailand, where most documents are written in Thai script, this could cause a problem, particularly if you can't read Thai. Few things annoy Thais more than someone who says, "What is this? I won't sign it unless I know what it is!"

If you and your wife are trying to buy a condo or car in her country and she passes documents to you and asks for your signature, just sign the darn things. Don't make her go through every point. It is fair to ask her for a brief explanation of the documents, but if you behave as if you don't trust her in front of a stranger and believe she is asking you to sign away your soul (or money in your savings account), then be prepared for more silent treatment, angry punching, sharp objects thrown at your head, or tears.

This advice is helpful for those working in Thailand too. If your office asks you to sign things, just sign them. They're trying to sort out your insurance, work permit, visa, accommodation pay, etc., and that means a lot of red tape and headaches they have to go through for you. All that hard work – and instead of receiving any thanks from you, you say, "I ain't signin' nut'n' 'less ya 'splainit tuh me!" The Thai rolls his or her eyes (actually you will see a smile or laugh, which often is the Thai equivalent) and says to him or herself: "This is just Western culture, calm down. The *farang* is just being paranoid like all other strange white people."

Another way to show distrust and paranoia is to always have the feeling that Thais want something from you every time they approach. This attitude doesn't have to be verbalized to be noticed. Your body language or lack of warmth among family or colleagues makes it clear. Yes, perhaps there are times that they might need something from you, but if you constantly keep everyone at arm's length, you'll never enter society and make lasting friendships. You may complain about the rent or electrical bill because there are many figures on it. But don't huff and puff and tell your wife that the Thais are tricky. The bill has been itemized and it's your fault if you cannot read the Thai description of each item. Go buy a Thai-language book!

As for a marriage, this distrust can cause serious problems. The Western man is always quick to blame his wife's family when she comes to him and asks for money. Let me stress that this topic must be dealt with before placing the ring on her finger, or you may have a very rough road ahead.

Try to get some idea from your wife how much she needs from you each month to help support her family. Do what you can and make it clear (in a polite way; remember, soft voice!) that you can't do more. Perhaps promise you can do more after you get a raise. Also, you can let your wife know your salary and monthly expenses. Yes, Thai women know that money does not appear out of thin air. If there is a discrepancy in what is available each month and what she needs to send to her family, then she will help you find ways to save money each month or try to find extra work for herself. Being open about finances will give her a strong platform to stand on when answering her family's request for more money and she will then know how to respond to a family member who comes to her. The point is that it's best to deal with this issue early, so you won't have to distrust her throughout your marriage and perpetuate her stereotype of the paranoid foreigner.

Distant from Family

Imagine you have already married your Thai sweetheart and one day she wants you to come along when visiting her family. Perhaps your Thai is not good enough to have any meaningful conversation, and the little English they might know is used to ask you personal questions regarding salary, when you'll have children, and whether you'll buy a house or condo (then they'll tell you exactly what you should do). Meanwhile, the matriarch is busy putting all kinds of fruits, snacks, and drinks in front of you, without asking if you are hungry or thirsty, and making assumptions about your inability to eat anything spicy. All this doesn't sound too appealing, so you beg your wife not to make you go, or even flat-out demand that you be allowed to spend some time at home while she goes alone.

For many Westerners the Thai relatives can be pushy and annoying. But you'll need to socialize with them for your marriage's sake. Thais already have the idea that Western families are not close. To Thais, 'close' doesn't necessarily mean emotionally; it often refers to physical proximity. Grandparents live with their children; a niece or nephew is sent to live with an uncle or aunt for a time because there is a better school where he or she lives. Siblings build houses next to each other. 'Close' in Thai also means that many family members are consulted or have a lot of influence in a young person's major decisions: what university to attend, which major to choose, who to marry, where to work and which house to buy. So if you boast to your potential Thai in-laws that you made decisions independently for your own life and that you got to where you are now without help, especially from your parents, be prepared for odd stares. Your accomplishments may make you seem an undesirable fit for their family. I can't think of any Thai folk songs or proverbs celebrating the 'self-made man.'

To avoid the stereotype of being distant, you're going to have to tag along on family visits sometimes. If your in-laws are constantly trying to feed you things you don't particularly like, drop hints with your wife beforehand. She'll then be able to pass on your requests to her parents that you are unable to eat certain foods, especially durian! Dropping hints with third parties is probably the best way to get things across in Thai culture. Let your wife know in a calm and uncomplaining manner and she will relay your hints to the appropriate family members, also in an indirect manner. There is always hope that someday, at some point, your in-laws will be able to adjust to you.

When they want to discuss those major life decisions you've made, such as university and work, maybe mention how a parent or uncle had

offered advice to you and you really took that advice to heart before you went ahead with a decision. Those odd stares will be replaced with smiles and nodding heads.

Stingy

Now we've come to probably one of the worst tags or labels in Thai culture. Stinginess is not something you want to be known for. But you should not take this to mean that you always have to be a pushover.

Think of your own culture. Westerners value independence. In everything you do you want to show people that you are capable, skilled, able to do things on your own. This is what you strive to show your family, your colleagues, your superiors. What if one day you completely lose your independence? You find yourself living with your parents again and needing their financial support to supplement your moonlighting income from your busboy job and help pay for the insurance payments on your run-down Japanese compact car because most of your salary goes to pay alimony. Pathetic indeed.

Well, as much as you don't want this to happen, so a Thai does not want to be known as a tightwad. Thais strive to show themselves to be generous just as the Westerner wants to be seen as strong and independent. How does this pertain to your marriage with your Thai wife? Well, by occasionally showing yourselves (as a couple) as generous with her family, you're fulfilling her basic cultural need for self-esteem. If you deny her this, just think how you would feel if someone took your independence away from you. For a Westerner, doesn't your independence provide you with self-esteem? Then who are you to prevent your Thai bride from gaining her own self-esteem, just because she, as a Thai, will find it through other means?

So how will your wife show generosity? Don't fear, most acts of generosity can be small, and usually stay within your budgets. It can mean paying for ice cream when you and friends meet at the ice cream parlor, going the extra kilometer when dropping them off at a bus station that is more convenient for them, or sharing with them something that you have. The little things done in Thai culture add up exponentially.

Getting ready for the rest of your life

Start by not teaching her about money

4

The time during courtship

The time between the first sight of the woman of your dreams and the moment you accept some responsibility within the relationship – in other words, the yoke of bondage – is blissful. Once responsibility rears its ugly head, it's all downhill from there if you're not prepared! But let's spend as much time as we can within the happy times, the dating period.

You see a nice Thai woman. What do you do? The first rule is to never be too anxious or aggressive. Thais love to smile, and not when they mean to roll their eyes. So your first step is to wait for eye contact and seize your moment. Smile! Then turn your head away and look in another direction. This technique is great when on buses, the BTS, the metro, waiting in front of lifts, waiting at beauty salons, dentists' offices, or any place where both of you are stationary. After you have turned away, turn back and wait for eye contact to be reestablished. Then smile and turn away again. This shows you're friendly but not too aggressive. Interested but not needy, or horny.

You can look back to see if she continues taking glances towards you. If she does, you can move on to the next step. That's if there is a chance of seeing this particular person again. So if you work in the same building and often see her at the popular noodle stands in the nearby *soi* or coming and going from the lobby, you can plan everything out nicely. The next step is to actually speak to her. The best way is to try a phrase or two in Thai unless she indicates that she would like to stop and have a conversation! If she is walking towards you or is coming out of the lift that you are waiting at, then wet your lips and prepare to say "*Sawat dii khrap.*" Say it again the next day you see her, and the next. Then when you see her walking or milling around the office building, ask her "*Pai nai khrap?*" which means "Where are you going?" It's a phrase that is completely harmless and still shows that you are neither pushy nor desperate.

The next step is to ask for her name – "*Chue arai khrap?*" – when you see her again. By this point, you should be ready to have a conversation. Now, if you have been in Thailand for many years or you can speak Thai quite well, why are you reading this book? But that's okay! I have in mind the Westerner who knows some stock phrases in Thai, enough to order food, shop, and greet people, but is not sure how to go about finding the right Thai woman and developing a successful relationship. So if that's you, then after you ask for her name in Thai and get the opportunity to have a conversation with her, do so in English. See how much she knows. The more English she knows, the more educated she is, the more money she makes, and the less chance she'll screw you over to buy a new buffalo for the family farm.

Exchange pleasantries such as what work she does, whether she likes it, and what province she is from. Tell her the same details about you. Just give her an idea of who you are, then say goodbye. Yep, don't ask her out on a date, don't ask to walk her to her bus stop or ride the metro with her. Just give her a taste of your animal magnetism (I confess, my husband told me to use that term. I'd still like to know what it means. Something about being drawn to animals?).

I know I warned you about girls who are too eager to ask you to have dinner with them, but if you've gone this far, and especially if you've spread this out over at least a couple of weeks, then you can sit back a little bit and see if she will ask you to lunch first. If she does, it is completely permissible to go. She's not being too easy. She's just meeting you halfway. If she wants to see you for dinner and a movie, well, I'm a stickler for taking it slow. I'll let you be the judge. If you often see her with many girlfriends from the office during lunch hour, she might be a little shy to just go off and have lunch with a *farang* where everyone will see her. Be sensitive to that and consider the possibility that is the reason why she'd prefer to see you away from the office, after hours, rather than during lunchtime in full view of her peers.

Oh! Don't forget to ask for her mobile phone number!

So, you are at a so-so Thai restaurant, the sun is setting, and you are with her. Don't prematurely assume that she fancies you. It may just be she wants to be nice to you, have a friend, or practice English to improve her own language skills because she's got a promotion in mind. She may already have a boyfriend. So relax and let some time go by. Patience now can save you a lot of heartache later.

Guessing whether she's interested or not is exactly that, guessing! But below are some signs that may indicate that she is available and interested.

While you're having dinner together, does she leave to go to the toilet and come back with her make-up retouched? Good! That shows she cares about how she looks in front of you. Does she ask for your mobile phone number without you offering it to her? Another plus! Does she ask what you do during your free time? Where you go? And most importantly, *who* you go with? Wonderful! She's fishing to see if you're seeing someone else.

You need to look out for the negative signs, too. If you ask her what she normally does during her free time, where she goes, who she goes with, and she gives vague answers or tries to change the topic, then that's definitely a bad sign. It's not your prying that is turning her off. Prying is a Thai way of measuring someone up. Don't give up on the first bad sign. Near the end of your first dinner or lunch together, you may ask her for a 'real' date on a particular night. If she says she is "*mai wang*" (not free) and does not offer an alternative evening, that is another bad sign. Your hope is to hear her offer another night that she is free.

Another way to test her after your first time together is to send text messages to her mobile phone, or e-mails, and see how quickly she responds. Obviously, the more quickly she replies, the more interested she may be. But then again, this is all a guessing game until she clearly sets aside special time for you and things are moving quickly from friendship to something else.

Let's move on ahead a few weeks or months to when the two of you are officially in a relationship. What can you do to impress a Thai woman? The number one rule – remember this because it is a matter of life and death for your relationship – is NEVER FORGET HER BIRTHDAY! You will not believe the consequences if you do. We Thais hold the birthday to be a very special day in a person's life. It is a celebration of that person. If you forget that, you might as well forget about any other

It's definitely a suicide. It's her birthday today and we found no birthday card or present!

Michael of Portland, Oregon, fell in love with a young woman who came from a simple background. At first he was worried about his girlfriend loving him only to increase her social status or spending money. His advice is to see how your potential mate handles the money that she does have. One young woman he dated spent four months' salary on a brand-name pair of jeans and was desperate for cash for many months after that, begging him for more money or borrowing from friends. Rightly moving on, his next girlfriend – whose income wasn't much different than the first one – spent much less for a pair of jeans at the weekend market and proudly showed them off to him as if she had purchased a top brand. He knew he had found the right mate with the right attitude toward money, despite her humble background. Budgeting skills should be learned early in life. Michael says: "Don't try to teach your girlfriend about money because by the time you meet, her habits and attitudes have become firmly established."

plans you might have had. They have gone down the drain. Thai women have committed suicide because of forgotten birthdays. I cannot stress how important this is. For my husband and many other Westerners, they would prefer that their birthdays passed unnoticed. For a Thai, they want the cake, the card, and the present, no matter what their age. They need to be reassured that there are people who think about and care for them. For most Western men, screw it, right?

Here's another tip to help you score points while dating. Don't just eat and see movies together. Movies are a bad way to have first dates. You never get to talk. But as you may already know, being inside a movie theater certainly doesn't stop other Thais from talking.

Take her to markets like the Night Bazaar along Silom Road and Chatuchak and walk around. Notice the type of items that catch her eye. See what colors she fancies. No, I don't mean go on a shopping spree for her, but when special days come up like her birthday or your dating anniversary, or you just want to surprise her, choose her gift carefully. She will be putty in your hands if she knows how much time, effort, and consideration you put into her gift. For us Thais, 'practicality' is not all that important. My husband knows I enjoy a certain brand of skin lotion from the United States. So for many special occasions he would buy me products from this brand. I made a comment that he had already bought this for me before. He said, "But you could use it. You're almost out." True, but that didn't really impress me. Try to make each new gift original. Of course, you can still buy the practical gifts on top of the other ones! No one ever put a limit on the number of gifts that can be given for one birthday.

Finally, before I end this chapter, I want to give you the 'secret weapon' to grab a Thai girl's attention. It's actually quite simple. Be a pathetic, incompetent nerd who reads the Bangkok bus map upside down. You think I'm joking? Bring out your secret weapon (no, not *that* one!) when you think she's not giving you enough positive signals. Think of something you need to do in Bangkok and ask if she knows how to do it. For example, ask her where to buy pillows for your sofa, where to buy cheap software, where to shop for shoes, books, or toenail clippers. It doesn't matter what you are looking for. You don't actually have to need anything. Just ask her if she knows where to get a good price. Almost any

Thai woman will say, "Oh, I know! Let me show you," and she'll take you there personally. Congratulations, now you can spend more time with the woman of your dreams.

You never need to ask a Thai, "Can you help me…" Just say what you need and sit back and see if she offers to help. If you make yourself seem unable to survive in Thailand without her help, she'll go out of her way to help you. Thais are sympathetic towards the pitiful. Play the part of the sad foreigner who can't survive in her confusing but beautiful country without her help. And *that* is your secret weapon!

5

Wedding bells and naked ladyboys

It's time to move on and talk about the special ceremony you'll go through to signify that you take your sweetheart seriously and will make a lifelong commitment to her. You've made it through the courtship and you're ready to stand at the altar.

Since most Thais follow Buddhism (to various degrees), it's highly probable that the woman you've chosen is Buddhist. There are numerous sources that can detail the ins and outs of a Buddhist wedding ceremony, so I will not explain it here. What you need to know is that no matter what religion, a reception will follow the ceremony. The receptions are normally secular, so they would be similar no matter if the two of you have a Buddhist or Christian ceremony beforehand, and at first glance they may appear very Westernized. But just because the reception takes place in an international hotel, don't let that fool you.

Before we discuss the reception and what to expect, let's go over some of the dos and don'ts of wedding planning. In case you haven't already discovered through your own investigations, or in case you are absolutely new to Thailand, Thais like to be told what to do. We need someone to look up to at all times. Decision-making responsibility is not something that we strive for. Remember the meaning of "close" in Thai families in regards to decision-making? It's no different for weddings. There's protocol, there's tradition, and there's a planner that tells us exactly what to do. Rarely will you see a Thai bride actively participating in the planning of her wedding. She will just worry about looking pretty, and maybe choose the studio for the pictures (after seeking counseling from many people), but as for deciding who will stand where, decorations, what to say, etc, she will leave it to someone else.

Now, here is where the conflict will come in, in case you haven't already seen it coming. During rehearsals, you may have a bright idea and want to add your input (at this point, beware of anything you may think is "bright"). The wedding planner, your future family-in-law, and your fiancé's friends all look at you as if asking: how dare you speak? They're not interested in your strange idea on the procession (if it's a Western-style ceremony – no idiot would dare try to change the Buddhist-style ceremony, would they?). Your soon-to-be-bride will not come to your defense either. You are all alone. So just relax and let the wedding planner do her thing.

If you're having a Western ceremony and your family plans on coming to Thailand to participate, then you need to sit down with your wife weeks, if not months, ahead of time and talk about your expectations for the ceremony. The only way to survive this delicate time is to give, give, and give. In other words, take little if anything at all!

Even though we may call it a Western-style ceremony in Thailand, there will be many strange elements. First of all, at the front of the chapel room will be at least two large sofas. Yes, it will look like someone's living room. The sofas will not necessarily match the rest of the decorations. To the Western eye, this will be an eyesore. Next, you may find it strange that the ceremony will need an MC. Yes, we are discussing the ceremony, not the reception. There will be someone off to the side with a little podium and microphone, entertaining the audience with his smooth, silky voice as he tells the crowd who is coming down the aisle.

"And next we have the sweet little flower girl! Her name is Jeab and she's just four years old, but just look how gracefully she can toss those flower petals, folks!"

"Oh, wait. Is that the bride I see? Okay, musicians, hit it! As you can see, the bride is wearing a dress designed and cut by (insert studio name here) and she is being escorted by her father, a taxi driver…"

I'm exaggerating. But I understand that to the Westerner, having an MC announce the function, name and vital statistics of each member of the wedding party is a bit overkill. Unless you want to make your blushing bride lose face, keep your lips shut and curved into an inscrutable smile. If you can do that, you're practicing the Thai way of rolling the eyes.

Another act that you will not only see but participate in is asking for her parent's blessings at the end of the ceremony. After the vows have been exchanged and rings placed on fingers, you will step down off the

stage and make your way, hand-in-hand, to the sofas. Get down on your knees, press your palms together in a *wai* and place your hands and head into the waiting and open palms of her parents or other elders. They will speak a few blessings for you (lots of kids, lots of money). If your parents make the trip, it would be a great honor to have them follow this tradition as well. It's a wonderful way of showing respect and thanking your elders for their wisdom, love, and care, and your parents may enjoy the uniqueness of being involved in something so foreign.

Whatever you do before you reach this point, don't complain, don't pout, and never say anything like "But I'm paying for this!" You will only put a knife through your bride's heart.

Okay, you're married but it is not time to rush to the honeymoon suite just yet. You have the reception to conquer. You and your wife will have had more freedom to decide what happens at the reception. There will be speeches, cake-cutting, cake-serving (to the elders), singing, and any other entertainment that you and your wife decide to add. But beware of the naked ladyboys!

You think I'm joking? I'm not. I said you'll have more control over what happens during the reception, but I didn't say you will have complete control. It's Thai tradition to sneak in something very risqué, or as my husband likes to say: raunchy! My husband was scared to death before our reception because he was afraid someone would plan something to embarrass us.

His fear was not unfounded. Before he knew me, he went to a Thai co-worker's wedding reception party. Out of two hundred people or more, he and a few other colleagues were the only foreigners. They were seated at the largest table, in front of everyone. They felt like trophies because they were not that close to the bride. Between speeches that they did not understand, half a dozen transsexuals came out on stage and started dancing to some heavy-rhythm music. Soon their dancing turned to stripping. And within minutes, five stark-naked ladyboys, pubic hair and all, were prancing around on stage. After they finished they put on some shorts (still topless) and went into the crowd to ask for tips. You can imagine the easy prey that was seated up front just below the stage: the five unsuspecting *farangs*. The ladyboys pawed and fawned over them. "You give me tip, honey!"

My husband is quite conservative, but he had very liberal colleagues. Even the unabashed, flamboyant gay friend was appalled as he threw a glance at my husband as if to say, "help me out of this," while a ladyboy had his hands inside his shirt, rubbing his nipple.

Needless to say, my husband and his colleagues were first to leave, as soon as the ladyboys gave up and went to other tables. But that night scarred my husband forever. He almost refused to have a reception party. But I assured him that since our wedding reception was to be held at a five-star hotel and his colleague's was at a run-down community center, we certainly would not have any naked former-men running around on stage.

But we were still in for a surprise. It was unavoidable. It wasn't anything like the naked ladyboys but still tasteless in my husband's opinion. A family member of mine had a neighbor's eight-year-old daughter do a Britney Spears-type dance with all the gyrating and hip action that is, well, not appropriate for an eight-year-old. His family did not make it to Thailand for the wedding, so he was saved from that humiliation, and we had it edited from the video, so no harm done.

If all this intrigues you to the point where you want to see how far someone will go to add shock value to your reception party, then you don't need to do anything except wait. But if you do not want something tasteless or shocking to interfere with your elegant reception, then make it very clear to your bride. Then speak with the MCs of the reception (there will be two Masters of Ceremonies, one for the ceremony, the other – usually two working together – for the reception). Give them a list of events that will happen during the reception, as planned by you and your wife, and tell them that under no circumstances must they give up the stage for someone not on the list. If someone does try to persuade them to give up the stage, have them call you and your wife over to see what the intruder is up to.

If your wedding is more on the Thai-traditional side, you should know that the parents are the most important people at the wedding, even more so than the bride and groom. The sofas are for them, they are paraded around the reception. In a Western wedding, people are there to celebrate the married couple. The bride's father might be the only one with anything to do during the ceremony: giving away the bride. And maybe the mothers light candles. Usually the groom's father appears useless and unimportant in that he traditionally doesn't have anything to do at the ceremony. But for Thais, the focus is on the parents. So you will have to balance all of these factors when getting married and keep smiling. Just remember that no one cares what you think, even though you are out no less than 125,000 baht for the wedding and reception.

If you are thinking this is too much – What about your culture? What about your family's traditions? – the answer to this goes back to what I have said and will say again in this book. You will have the best chance for a successful relationship if you find a Thai woman with some knowledge and understanding of the world outside Thailand. A person like this will be more open and willing to compromise. And compromise is one of the most important ingredients after forgiveness for a successful relationship.

6

The price of the bride

I told you this book was not necessarily organized in chronological order. I chose to arrange it topically instead because the discussion of the dreaded dowry is best left until after the wedding and reception.

Of all issues, this one is the thorniest for Westerners. From your point of view, the dowry is probably an outdated practice involving payment for a bride, a horrible act that treats the bride as a commodity, or a despicable reason for the bride's family to unfairly prosper from the love-struck groom. For some, it is acceptable but still an annoying duty that puts one in a burdensome financial situation.

For many Thais, it is an honor. It is another means to show generosity and fulfill the basic human need for self-respect. Also, we are showing thanks to the bride's parents for raising her and educating her. Yes, I know what you are thinking: "Shouldn't her parents raise and educate her out of love? Why do they need to be repaid for this?"

This is just the way things are. Here lies the problem: earlier I suggested finding the most educated Thai woman you can. The benefit of this is that she can earn more money and if her parents have the same status, they'll be less dependent on her, and you! However, this may cost you more when dealing with the dowry. The more educated she is, the higher the price of the dowry will be.

You may be lucky and find a woman with a family so familiar with Western culture that they don't worry about a dowry. Or you may find a Thai-Chinese woman (in this situation, the parents immediately give back more than you gave to them). But if the dowry is expected and you show your disdain for such a request, then expect trouble. Your wife will lose face. Her devotion to you may wane and your acceptance into the family will be somewhat superficial.

Don't worry, there's an answer! Here's the trick for those young men who are still paying off student loans or making car payments and don't have a lot of money saved up, and can't go to their parents and ask for money to pay the five-figure dowry of their well-educated Thai bride. The trick in dealing with the dowry is to let go of the money with the feeling that it is nothing more than an investment for yourself, or at least for your wife. For example, one Western man offered to buy (finance, actually) his future mother-in-law a new house. The monthly payments for a house in Thailand are quite reasonable and easy to handle even on a Thai salary. The catch was this: The house had to be in the wife's name only, not the mother's. The mother said yes. Why not? It was not the money she needed but the face in front of relatives and neighbors. The neighbors would see that she had a new house (it was not revealed that the house was in the wife's name or that it was financed) and she would gain face. The husband feels that he is investing in property. When the house is paid for and the mother has passed away, they will have a retreat in northern Thailand. So the husband pays the mortgage without a complaint. Even if there wasn't a dowry to consider, any husband would want to invest in something, so there's nothing to complain about.

So if paying for a dowry is a real turnoff for you, then be creative and look for a need that her parents may have. Look for something that will benefit you and your wife. Dowries don't have to be cash. They can become investments for your future and more face for your in-laws.

Besides property, consider insurance. This is good especially if your wife's family is lower on the social status and income pole. They probably don't have investments for retirement or good health insurance. Unless hard cash is in desperate need and that's the only asset your future in-laws understand, visit an international assurance company with your wife and look through some plans. You can find a life insurance policy for both of your wife's parents that pay the surviving spouse after one of them passes on. Other plans return money to you after so many years. Your in-laws will gain face with the other villagers because they have something so 'sophisticated' as life insurance at an amount three times what they'd see their entire lives while working. Include your wife as a beneficiary for the last remaining parent. You pay for the plan for so many years and eventually your investment makes a return. So put away those harsh feelings regarding a dowry and try to find a way to make it benefit you and your wife.

Living together

If a guest uses our bathroom to wash his or her hands and sees the toilet seat down, I may lose my reputation.

7

"Mai wai laew!"

"I can't take this any more!"

There's a song that talks about the "little things" that drive someone crazy. There are so many rude, horrible things you can do to a person and they can let it slide, but small things like talking in the movie theater can make that person's blood boil. I remember listening to a small group discussion in which the speaker was American. In the group was an Arab man who kept yawning loudly. He was very active and was participating in the discussion, but would yawn loudly. I could see the American's face pause just a moment to collect himself when a loud yawn filled the small room. It was rather funny when you consider that to an American and most Westerners, yawning loudly does not mean that you are just tired. It means that you are bored! But for Arabs, they don't make this connection between boredom and a noisy yawn.

In this chapter I'm going to talk about the habits Thai girls have that may make your skin crawl. The Thai girl of your dreams may exhibit some of these habits, so it is good that you know what to expect.

I'm not going to discuss the idiosyncrasies (my husband obviously helped me with this word, but this time I DO understand what it means) that an individual may have – like forgetting to put the toilet seat down (something my husband always fusses about) or not putting empty clothes hangers back in the closet (which I always yell at my husband for). I mean things that could be due to cultural differences. Things that Thais would not think twice about, but Westerners would.

Using my own marriage as a reference point, some annoying habits that my husband likes to complain about involve the use of a mobile phone, watching TV together, the way we Thais walk, the way we choose where to stop and talk or park our grocery cart that blocks paths and walkways, and travel an hour from home to buy something that is a few baht cheaper than what we could get five minutes away from home. These 'annoying' things we do are a part of being Thai.

The first powder keg is the mobile phone. I remember when only those with money had mobile phones. They were over-priced and seen as a status symbol. I know now that things have changed because one day I was walking in Bangkok and there was a street sweeper in front of me. I heard the stifled ring of a mobile phone and suddenly the street sweeper stopped sweeping and reached in her blue/orange vest and pulled out a mobile phone. Nowadays you cannot escape them. They are everywhere, and because of this they interrupt every human function or gathering. Whether it is a classroom, church service, political speech, or a session of wild coupling, the ringing tones of mobile phones will be present and divert the attention of those participating in such events.

A habit you might find many Thai women exhibiting is the urge and constant need to pick up every phone call, no matter what she is doing or doing it with. Stay a day in my condo and you'll hear my husband's most frequent expression: "You don't *have* to answer it." Many times we are on the sofa watching a video and my mobile phone rings. I jump to

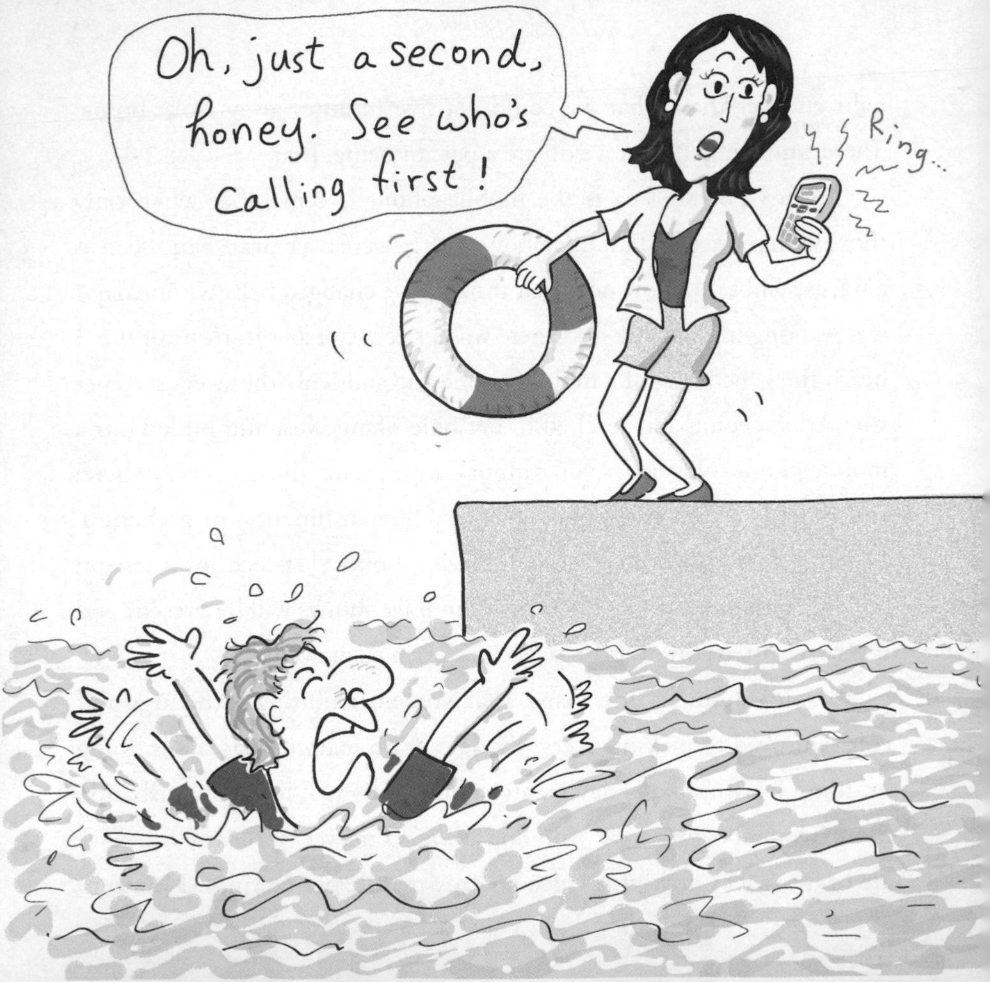
Oh, just a second, honey. See who's calling first!
Ring...

get it and immediately my husband gets upset. Before my hand reaches the phone, I hear him reminisce how his father would say, "Don't answer it!" whenever the phone would ring while his family was watching *The Dukes of Hazzard.*

My husband has not been able to break me from this habit. While we are having a serious discussion, I break it off to answer my mobile and talk with a friend, who I had just spoken to an hour before, about nothing in particular. When we are arguing, I answer my mobile. When we are being affectionate, I answer it. I cannot let it go. I don't know why. Mobile phones are an addiction for women. We just feel the need to reach out and gossip about someone. According to one research study, women speak three thousand more words than men per day! On the other end of that wireless signal is another female with some banal information to tell. And I have to hear it. The example from my own life is no different than other Thais. On top of this, few Thai women bother looking at the caller ID or care to. We have caller ID to help us decide whether we want to answer it or not. But we never use it. We may look, but we answer anyway, even if we don't really want to talk to that individual.

If you can accept our quirks with mobile phones, then I'll have to warn you about watching TV or videos together. I always thought it strange when watching a movie with my husband that he would press pause whenever I would stand up and leave the sofa. Maybe I was just going to the kitchen to get a drink, a snack, or wanted to go to the bathroom for a moment. I realized that this was cultural when I visited the States and his family and friends did the same thing. As soon someone said, "I have to use the bathroom," the person with the remote would press pause. I guess my husband sees watching TV and videos as a group experience. The group is bonding even without any words being exchanged between the group members. In the West, the host wants the others to enjoy the story as much as he or she does.

For Thais, the act of watching TV together is not so concordant; it is not seen as a shared experience. At least not to the point where the show must be stopped if one member's attention is momentarily diverted.

to l...

"Mai wai laew!"

And we certainly wouldn't ignore our ubiquitous mobile phones belting out ringtones from Beethoven to the sexy, naughty, bitchy Tata Young.

This can be really frustrating if you want to share a memorable or favorite movie with your Thai sweetheart. My husband often rents DVDs of his favorite movies and wants me to watch them with him and have the same emotional experience. He would spend days or weeks talking about a particular title he was going to rent. Then when we had a free evening, he would bring it home. Twenty minutes into the movie my mobile phone would ring, I move towards it, and immediately he feels great disappointment in my apparent lack of enthusiasm for the movie he feels passionate about.

It is not that Thais are not interested in the movie or TV show. Even during a really sappy, addicting Korean soap opera we will jump to answer our mobile phone, even if the phone had been left in another room. Of course I want to share the joy or sadness of my husband's favorite movies with him. But I'm Thai, and I'm addicted to my mobile phone. So I am *greng jai*, meaning I'm afraid of irritating my husband if I were to ask him to stop the movie and wait for me. I don't want

...errupt his viewing pleasure. But, as we can see, this can have the opposite effect.

Have you ever walked in a shopping center, or market, or a crowded sidewalk with many Thais walking along with you? Have you noticed that when you try to walk past a Thai, it's as if they gravitate towards you just before you pass them, resulting in a blocked path for you? Thais don't walk in straight lines! The strangest thing is that we somehow know when someone is about to pass us, then we drift to the area in front of them. So the poor person whose only sin is that they happen to walking faster must try to pass on the other side. The Thai person in front of them then drifts to the other side and blocks their path again. Plenty of Westerners have huffed and puffed while trying to maneuver around a sidewalk full of Thai people. Now I find myself doing the same thing: huffing and puffing and rolling my eyes. Perhaps this is part of our nature: not to hurry, take our time, don't be serious, even when walking. We'll eventually arrive at our destination. Meanwhile, we just enjoy the leisurely stroll. It's the Westerners who have to walk in straight lines, thinking of only the destination with no regard to what they'll find before reaching it.

Speaking of blocking paths, there's another Thai trait. The basic unwritten rule is to park your shopping cart in the aisle or car in the alley in a way that takes up as much space as possible so people cannot go around you. My husband has been patient for quite some time, but now I hear him mumbling complaints while grocery shopping – "Yeah, that's a good place to park your cart, idiot!" Theoretically there should be enough room for two carts to pass by each other in an aisle. But at times the store will place a display of green tea or potato chips along one side, leaving room for only one cart to go by. If a Thai wants to stop and look at something on the shelves within the area of the display, will they stop the cart in front of or behind the display, out of the way of other shoppers? Nope, the cart will go between the display and the opposite shelves. So now the aisle is completely blocked. It doesn't just happen in grocery stores, it's everywhere you go. Why does this happen? Something has to happen because people are coming and going. So who is to say that the "normal" thing is to be considerate of others and make sure your cart's not blocking someone else's path?

The next cultural habit to discuss is, I'm proud to say, not one that I am guilty of. But many Western men will have met Thais who will go out of their way to save a few baht. Saving money is actually a good thing, it would seem. But for Thais, they'll spend two or three hours traveling across town to save "a few baht." Now how many coins would you have to save to make it worth spending the extra time? That is up to you, but the amount the Thais think is far below what most Westerners would say. It could be as little as ten baht! Yes, a Thai might live near Seacon Square, and find a souvenir that she wants to give to her boss, but her friend next to her will say, "Oh, I saw that at Chatuchak for much less. Here it is *pang maak* (expensive)." So they'll rush out and catch a bus (or even a taxi!) and make their way to Chatuchak from Seacon Square, covering a distance that is further than most Bangkokians' daily commute to work. She will find exactly what she found at Seacon Square, and yes, her friend was right. It IS cheaper – 25 baht cheaper. Meanwhile, the air-conditioned bus ride for two costs 50 baht. Or the taxi ride costs 121 baht. But she's still happy that she found it for a lower price.

This may sound irrational or just plain crazy, and you may be right, but what was the girl's point in doing this? Was it to save money? If it were, then yes, it does seem irrational to the logic-loving Western man. But in fact, saving money was not the point. If she had purchased the souvenir at Seacon Square, her shopping time would have been over. But she had more things to say to her friend, more people to gossip about, more time to waste, more places to see. So we see that she decided to go somewhere else to buy the item *just so* she could prolong her day with her friend. She didn't want to go home so quickly or have to think of another reason to shop. If she had stayed at Seacon Square and didn't want to go home, she would have shopped more and spent more. So, financially, it didn't matter that she spent money traveling to Chatuchak, as four times that amount would have been spent on Starbucks coffee or a meal at McDonald's while they sat and gossiped. You may think Thai women do things irrationally, but when you consider the true reasons behind their actions, they are just as rational and no more wasteful with their money. Of course, you might say there's no reason to go shopping in the first place. But then for the woman, there would be no more reason to live!

The last cultural habit I will discuss is the *apparent* inability of Thais to say 'I don't know.' Picture the poor farang trying to find a shop that will sell a tool to help him fix his leaky faucet. He goes to a shop and explains what he wants (let's say he has reasonable Thai language skills). The store employee says the store doesn't carry that item. He asks where he could find it. The employee points him in the "right" direction. So off he goes, walking in circles. After a while he stops at a hair salon and asks if someone there might know where to find the hardware store that the first shop told him about. They point him in another direction. So off he goes again. He's passed a 7-11, a massage parlor, three more hair salons, a couple of noodle stands, but still no hardware shop. He asks a group of motorcycle taxi drivers about the shop. They chat amongst themselves and say it's on such-and-such street just a few more blocks away. The farang huffs and puffs because he was just in that area but couldn't find

P'Tum in Bangkok has some good advice for quarreling couples. In her marriage, she finds that it's healthier for the couples to separate when moody or angry. One person should not try to convince the other of his or her point, but wait until both have been alone with their thoughts before coming together again.

Noot of Chiang Mai, who is married to a German, says that a husband or wife should not make the other partner feel like a loser in a discussion, nor act like a winner. She says every success and every failure of communication is due to the effort or fault of both people, not just one of them.

it. So he tells a motorcycle boy to take him there. But they don't. They just smile and say it is too difficult to reach. By now, the farang should be getting the hint that there's no hardware shop in the area at all. So why didn't the Thais he had encountered say so? Why couldn't anyone say "I don't know"?

These types of verbal exchanges happen every day in Thailand. For every question you ask, there is a smiling Thai ready with an answer. It may not be the most honest or correct answer, but it's an answer that they think you will want to hear. Thais don't just avoid saying "I don't know" to foreigners; they do this to their own too. I've been led down *sois* and through shophouses plenty of times looking for something that is not there. I myself am guilty of giving my husband an answer to his question when actually I have no clue. Then he gets frustrated and says "If you don't know, just say so!"

It's a hard habit to overcome. The reason is maybe we are too shy to say we don't know, or we don't want to see the disappointment on the person's face when we can't help them find what they want. Or perhaps we honestly believe if we just send them in some direction, they will eventually meet with someone who DOES know the answer.

I'll have to take a moment and defend the Thais regarding this matter. Foreigners like to blame us for this inability to admit our ignorance. Actually, this reveals the foreigner's ignorance of the Thai language. Thai people actually do say "I don't know" every day! Whereas Westerners say "I don't know" in the answer, Thais say it in the question.

In Thai, when we need to ask for information, we begin our request with the phrase *"mai sap wa."* Translated into English, it means "I don't know." The *"wa"* is just a particle word to connect the admission of ignorance with the topic that we are asking about. Listen to Thais approach each other in shopping centers and stores and you will definitely hear this expression.

"I don't know if this department store has a Starbucks" really means, "Where is a Starbucks?"

"I don't know what time you close" means, "What time do you close?"

"I don't know where I can find a hardware store" means, "Where is a hardware store?"

So, accusing Thais of not being able to say "I don't know" is unfair and uncalled for. We say it all the time. But we are so used to admitting it in the question that it seems too odd for us to put it in the answer.

Only those strange people from a strange culture we call "Westerners" would dream of saying "I don't know" in an answer.

8

Bathroom etiquette and poop chutes

We've discussed annoying habits that you'll find in many Thai women. To add some balance, let's look at the Western man. One of the biggest pet peeves that I have with my husband is what he does NOT do in the bathroom. He comes from a country, like many other Western countries, that gets buried in snow for many months out of the year. People don't sweat where he comes from like they do in Thailand, so he is used to taking one shower per day. It took me a long time to push and push him to take two showers in Thailand. His normal shower time was in the morning, but he would want to come to bed (and, yuck, touch me) without showering, instead relying on the cleaning he had done earlier in the day.

Thailand is dirty. It's hot. Two showers may not be enough, especially in Bangkok. If you come from cold climates and normally don't take a shower at night, you need to change that habit.

Despite Thailand being so dirty, or maybe because of it, Thais value cleanliness. We don't like to see dirt on ourselves. Dirt on the streets, trash on the sidewalks, and mangy dogs in our pathways are okay, but make sure you scrub yourself clean. One reason why we do not value the beauty of dark-skinned girls so much is because we associate the dark skin with being dirty. I know that's not true; dark skin does not mean a lack of hygiene or skin care, but this belief is part of the Thai psyche. Anyway, if you refuse to take a shower before bed, don't be one bit surprised to find yourself sleeping alone. To the Thai woman, it's equivalent to blowing your nose at the dinner table or clearing the phlegm from your throat at a business meeting. It is unbearably disgusting to her.

Another pet peeve, and this one causes a really bad smell, is how Westerners clean themselves after defecating. Sitting on a toilet during my first visit to America was a bit of a culture shock. When I finished, I leaned around for a hose to spray my backside (you wouldn't believe the time I spent searching for the appropriate terms for this topic) and to my shock there was no hose or nozzle. So how could I clean myself? All that was available was toilet paper.

Maybe toilet paper is enough to clean oneself in cold climates, but it is not enough in Thailand. Your private parts will not be clean enough. We attach hoses and spray nozzles to our commodes for a reason. Use them! I can't tell you how exasperating it is to try to be romantic and frisky with my husband only to find bits of toilet paper sticking out of his ass!

My husband, like many Western men, just can't bear the thought of grabbing a water hose and sticking it up his poop chute (I heard that on TV and thought it had a cute ring to it) and squeezing the nozzle. He says he does not want the trouble of getting dry enough to put his pants back on. Yes, even shitting can be a source of culture shock in Thailand. The problem is that in the heat of a tropical climate, if you do not spray yourself, your butt will begin to smell. The smell will seep into your underwear, whether they are briefs or boxers, and the smell will linger, even after washing them. I wash and wash my husband's boxers, but I still smell it. Granted, I have to put my nose into his boxers to smell the offending odor, and most people do not bury their noses into someone else's underwear, but let's be honest, it's destined to happen at some point for a couple in a deep relationship.

Fortunately for me, my husband does use the water hose in our shower stall to spray that particular area, so it does get a good cleaning at least once a day, but the best way to have good hygiene is to do it in the bathroom stalls whenever you defecate. It's not so bad. I would think some people out there might enjoy the sensation of cold water shooting up their butt!

Another upsetting habit for a Thai woman is where the foreign husband places the tissue after wiping himself. For Thais it's not a problem. We

spray so we only need a piece of tissue paper for dabbing ourselves dry. There's a garbage bin by the toilet where we throw the damp tissue, and there are no embarrassing, smelly brown stains to worry about. But for the Western man who has yet to master the water hose and has to use four or five rolled pieces of toilet paper to rub their anus raw, they face a dilemma: do they put the toilet paper, now filled with as much crap as there is floating in the toilet, in the garbage bin? Hopefully not! The next Thai person would not appreciate the sight when they open the lid to throw away their own toilet paper. So the Western man throws all that paper into the toilet. The problem is that the pipes used for plumbing in Thailand are not as wide as those used in most Western countries.

Our toilet has been blocked many times because my husband throws his wads of tissue paper in there. One time it took a week, many bags of sodium, two bottles of chemicals, and many attempts with a plunger to get it unblocked. It was a nightmare. We could not use our toilet for many days. When we tried to flush it, the contents would flow over. I was tired of complaining to my husband about this. So I told him, "You will clean this up!" And he did. And to this day he does not throw tissue paper in the commode. Having to deal with his own shit, literally, broke him of this habit by making him realize how tight us Thai girls' pipes are.

We compromised: he doesn't have to spray his backside, which means I still have to deal with his bumtags, but he empties the bin after every episode in the bathroom and replaces it with a new plastic bag immediately. And compromise is what makes a marriage work!

I don't want to return to the bathroom after this chapter, so I'm going to bring up this one last topic: the toilet seat. Here is another cultural difference that may cause some strain. My husband is a stickler for a closed-seated toilet. He marches me back into the bathroom to close the seat after I leave it up, which I do constantly. Thais want the seat up. Why, you may ask? Simple. When we see a toilet seat in the down position, it can only mean that the toilet is so dirty that we are shy for our guests to see it.

My husband responds by asking why anyone would want to stare at the bottom of a commode. Remember that a Thai is worried about how things look, not how they really are.

If a guest uses our bathroom to wash his or her hands and sees the toilet seat down, I may lose my reputation. That guest may think I do not keep my toilet clean – even though the guest did not open the lid to take a peek or a leak!

9

The sniff

You may have noticed by watching Thai movies or television or by observing couples in public that Thais do not kiss the way Westerners do. We don't even peck one another on the cheeks. Kissing can be a way to greet one another in Europe, like my French friends do to me when we get together a couple of times a year, or it can be a hot, sexy interlude between two lovers, with tongues intertwined, mixed with grunting noises. You will not find this in Thailand unless it is between a sex tourist and a bar girl who has completely removed herself from Thai norms and values.

Thais have what we call the sniff. It looks like we are smelling one another (again, maybe this is something that reveals our beliefs about hygiene and cleanliness). We press our noses against the loved one's cheek, but not too hard, and give a slight sniff. This is our special Thai way of showing affection. Much different from French kissing, isn't it.

You don't necessarily have to try sniffing your Thai wife's cheek, but I'm sure she would appreciate the gesture sometimes. Once a Thai woman gets accustomed to French kissing, she will enjoy doing that with you, I'm sure (in private, of course). But there will be a special tingle in her heart and a sincere smile will come to her face if you try to show her that you have mastered the sniff too.

10

Mocking

This topic could have come under the heading of annoying habits that your loved one might exhibit, but it deserves its own chapter. Thais love to mock each other. When they mock it is not so serious. 'Tease' might be a more appropriate word, but when you hear the things they tease about, you will want to label it mocking. Mocking is done in all peer and romantic relationships, but is not appropriate between subordinates and superiors.

Skin tone and weight are two popular topics that Thais bring up. By skin tone, I mean dark-complexioned skin tone, as we do not make fun of white-skinned girls… of course. Thais can be sensitive about their weight too, but that doesn't stop them from teasing each other about their chubby thighs and fat cheeks, both sets.

Let me use my husband's experience as an example. There were two girls in a class he was teaching. One was overweight, one was not. There was some light bantering between them, my husband said, but then the lighter one shouted at the heavier one: "You fat evil pig!" My husband froze, expecting to have to deal with tears and sobs from the heavier one. She jumped up and pointed at the other girl and said something about a buffalo. Then that was it. Finished. The class laughed and they went on. My husband saw these two afterwards become good friends. They were freshmen at the time but still were together in the same social group as seniors. He was amazed that this could be said in a classroom and the overweight student not take offense.

Well, I can't say the overweight one was not offended. She may have cried when she went home that night, who knows. But in Thai society, we're not to take offense when a friend teases us like that. At least we're not to react in public. That would cause both parties to lose face. We're

supposed to smile, laugh along, as though we were saying, "Yep, I'm one fat ugly evil pig!"

I have my own horrible experience with mocking. I mocked a member of my husband's family. We were visiting America and I patted one young member of the family on the stomach and said with a big Thai smile, "You have a belly." For the next couple of days I noticed something was weighing heavy on my husband's mind. I can tell when he has something to say but doesn't want to bring it out in the open. Finally he reminded me during the family get-together that his nephew left suddenly. I remembered. Well, my husband said, he was offended and embarrassed by what I had said to him.

I was horrified. I certainly didn't want to hurt anyone's feelings. I cried and cried. My mother-in-law told me not to worry about it. Eventually I had the chance to apologize over the matter and my apology was accepted. But in my mind I still can't stop myself from saying, 'Why make a mountain out of a mole hill?' Or ask, 'What is your problem?' But I can't do that. Americans, and I would say most Westerners, are more sensitive about these issues, but Thai friends will not express so much anger when teased on such a matter. It's bad for everyone if they do, because they will feel uncomfortable and we don't want to make others feel that way. If we do, we shame ourselves.

I'm sure you will hear Thais tease their darker-skinned friends constantly. It's an understatement to say that most dark-skinned Thais are ashamed of their skin. It's no wonder that you see so many advertisements for skin-whitening cream. This fascination with white skin goes back centuries, so it will not be extracted from the Thai mentality anytime soon, but there are efforts to increase the self-worth and positive image of dark skin in Thai society. Unfortunately, a lot of these efforts turn into more mockery such as the Miss Dark Thailand beauty pageants.

The biased attitude towards dark skin has to do with social classes, with a mixture of immigration trends and the mixing of races. In the past, and it is still true today, the lower classes worked outside in the fields and as laborers. They were constantly in the sun. Their skin became very dark. They were usually dirty because of their work with mud and dust. So Thais began associating dirt with dark skin and lower social classes. This still permeates Thai society today. People of darker skin are usually considered of lower class, even if their clothes and mannerisms suggest otherwise. In contrast, the aristocrats and business people stayed inside and protected their skin. They stayed white.

Another factor is the more recent immigration of the Chinese. Typically whiter than the Southeast Asians, they settled, started businesses, became successful and rich, and the association of white skin with success and riches help solidify this biased attitude. A third reason may simply be that we as humans always want what we don't have. Since most Thais are dark-complexioned when compared to Europeans, we tend to want to be whiter, different from the masses. Why do white people want to be tanned? If only we could be satisfied with what we have!

My husband once met a Thai friend he hadn't seen in a while and commented, "You're darker." She did not take the comment the way he intended. He meant that she was prettier (in his eyes), but a Thai will not think that way. So be careful when you remind someone they are dark. It should only be said to a close friend, if at all.

Maprang is from Pattani in the south of Thailand, where people are normally very dark-complexioned. When she came to study and work in Bangkok, she felt shy about her skin color and it even made her lose confidence. Despite the attention she received from foreign men, she never felt beautiful. She did marry a nice foreign gentleman who raved about her dark skin. But to her, his words sounded like he was mocking her. She suggests not overacting or mentioning your woman's dark skin too often. You can make her feel beautiful in other ways. Compliment her hair style, her dress sense, or her figure. Not every Thai woman is as sensitive as Maprang, but for many women it takes time to get used to the fact that their foreign man is turned on by their skin color – while at the same time they are the butt of many jokes within their own society.

11

Exaggerations and understatements

Thais hate being the bearers of bad news. You will not know the lengths that we will go to avoid giving information or answers that will likely disappoint the one who needs the information. In a previous chapter I mentioned that Thais don't like to say "I don't know." But it goes much deeper than this. Thais tend to exaggerate or understate the facts to almost all sensitive issues. Money is certainly one of them.

My husband often asks me for the price of something we need to buy. For example, we needed a fax machine. He asked how much it would cost. I gave him a reasonable figure that he considered and said it wouldn't be a problem. Okay, I didn't lie! I wasn't sure how much a fax machine would cost. But it is my habit to give the lowest amount possible. We went to the store and yes, we did find a fax machine that cost close to my estimate. But it was the cheapest in price and the cheapest in quality. We knew the features we needed and the cheapest models did not have them, so we continued looking and found the fax machines that carried those features; they were twice or triple my estimate. My husband was a little frustrated. He thought he could have gotten a good fax machine for a low price but ended up spending much more.

Now some sneaky Thai women will use this technique to get their husbands in the store. Once they are in there, they see that the prices are higher than expected, and they decide to leave; but the wife will do her best to convince them that since they are there, they should look seriously. And she persuades him to spend more. That certainly wasn't my intention. Maybe I'm not familiar with prices of electronics, and maybe that is the case with most other Thai women too. But I will try to think of the lowest figure I can that sounds reasonable.

My husband understood my figure to be an estimate of a mid-range fax machine. And when Westerners talk about price and cost, I think that's what they do: what is the average price? But if you receive an estimate from your wife, bear in mind that you will have to add a lot more.

The same goes for distance and time. My husband now refuses to take directions from me when we drive. We often have to run errands around Bangkok and go to streets we are not familiar with. One day we had to go across town from Sukhumvit Soi 103 to 'somewhere' on the north side. I told my husband to go to Ramindra that very morning. He had some idea of Ramindra Road and asked, 'Do we take the Minburi exit?' which meant that we would head east. I said, 'Yes,' just to say something, not really thinking (or knowing) where to go. I, like many other Thai women, would call the contact once we were in the area.

Off we went, reaching Ramindra Road 45 minutes later. We headed east and I told my husband 'We'll come to a roundabout, then turn right.' Being American, and never having seen a roundabout until visiting Asia, he wasn't too familiar with them. He asked, 'Turn right, you mean head south?' I nodded my head, confident that we would find the roundabout. Well, kilometer after kilometer passed and we never reached it. We passed Fashion Island and reached a three-way intersection. The traffic police blocked traffic from turning right so we had to turn left. Feeling a bit confused, my husband asked about the roundabout. I decided THIS was the appropriate time to call our contact (yes, I hear all you Western husbands snickering. Thais call when there is a snafu, not to avoid a snafu).

My contact mentioned the way to go and I saw a sign. I told my husband to follow it. The sign would take us west. "But you said head south at the roundabout," he protested. We drove and drove and never saw a roundabout. We agreed to head back the other way and look for that elusive roundabout. I had to call four or five times and we still weren't satisfied. Eventually we were back on Ramindra headed west. I decided THIS was the appropriate time to give him the detail I knew all along but was lazy to say: our destination was near the airport. "But you said Minburi!" my husband yelled. He saw a sign up ahead that said Lak Si and let out a long, deep breath. "I know that roundabout! If you had told me it was Lak Si in the first place, I would have gotten us there easily," he continued to yell.

So how did I understate? I told him to just go to Ramindra and then "ruey ruey," which means "just keep going in this general direction." No detail is given. No research of facts is carried out. And when you marry your Thai sweetheart, be prepared to be treated like a low-level spy. Everything is on a need-to-know basis and in due time!

Anyway, my husband won't get in the car now until I have called ahead for detailed directions. I'm proud to say that I am trying my best to find the details in the time that he demands (days and days ahead of time, which is crazy!). But it is a hard habit to break. God knows I'm trying.

Exaggerating and understating will be a daily part of your marriage. When dealing with figures and dollar amounts, don't take your wife's estimate at face value. Be suspicious. She's not being tricky on

purpose, she's being Thai. When you ask about the grocery bill, expect an understatement. How much did she save with coupons? Expect an exaggeration. How many weeks will your mother-in-law visit you if you live in your country? Expect an understatement. Plane ticket for your mother-in-law? Understatement. The gifts that she will bring with her for you two? Exaggeration. You get the picture.

12

Table manners

Eating together can be a common source of frustration. What you may feel are normal table manners may embarrass and frustrate your wife. No, you don't have to worry about placing your elbows on the table. Thais don't mind. They do it themselves. But, don't make noises with the cutlery and dishes. Whenever your fork, knife, or spoon makes contact with a dish and makes a noise, quickly say, "Excuse me." You might be separating food with the edge of a fork and it hits the plate, or you may be lowering your spoon into a soup bowl and you ding the edge of the bowl, or as you reach for a glass and bring it to your mouth, you hit the edge of a plate. All of these innocent mishaps are considered rude table manners and the perpetrator needs to ask to be excused.

Mind your teeth, too. Hitting your teeth with your fork or spoon is also a big turnoff for Thais. So, in other words, eat with as little noise as possible.

P'Daeng of Bangkok is a newlywed, but she has some advice to share with men wanting a Thai wife. Her husband commits an act that is considered rude to Thais. He constantly hits and scrapes his plate with his cutlery. Thais consciously avoid hitting their table setting, and if they do, they always say, "Excuse me." So, men, keep the noise down at the dinner table, and don't even think of playing "Jingle Bells" with the water glasses.

Don't leave the table just yet. There are a few more things that Westerners often do that may irritate the Thais, or embarrass your Thai wife if you eat in public or join a social gathering. Don't spend too much time stirring your food, such as twirling your spoon in a soup bowl or turning the rice on your plate over and over. These gestures can signify that something is wrong with the food and that you are trying to correct it.

A friend of ours, a Western man, was having dinner with his Thai girlfriend and her father. The father was paying for it, so the young man who was dating his daughter was the guest.

At the end of the dinner, the Western man stirred the ladle around in the pot a few times; for no reason, he exclaimed later on. He was just fidgeting at the table and was looking for something to touch. But his Thai girlfriend felt ashamed. She felt that his gesture meant that the amount of food her father had paid for was not enough and he was scrounging for more.

The conclusion here is that many of the Western rules of table manners will not apply to Thai society. However, you have a new set of rules to follow. Don't make noise and don't just pick up ladles or cutlery and poke at things on the table. Your Thai wife will give you the cold shoulder later.

Oh, and there's one more thing. Thais like to comment on food, so if you say nothing, it will be taken to mean that the food is not delicious. Always compliment the cook if that person is eating with you; if not, at least say something about how delicious the meal is.

13

Dressing in public

When I tell you that you need to watch what you wear in public, those of you who have been to Thailand are going to say that this chapter is hypocritical because you've seen Thai people wear worse things. True, but I'll be honest: because you are a foreigner, Thai society will expect a little more from you.

There's a danger you have to look out for when you are visiting or deciding to live in a foreign country. Whether you know it consciously or not, you will feel that many of your inhibitions have been left behind in your home country, and now that you are in Thailand, you are free as a bird to act and behave as liberally as you feel. Perhaps people feel this way because no one from their own culture is looking at them. Combine this with ignorance of Thai culture, where it may seem to the new Western visitor to the Land of Smiles that there are no rules at all, and the Western man will not care how he acts. He will feel invisible in Thai society. But there are rules. And though you see Thais breaking them, it doesn't mean that you can too. So put that burden of inhibitions back on your shoulder.

The first thing to avoid when dressing in Thailand is short pants, no matter how expensive or fancy they are. You will see hundreds of people in Thailand wearing shorts. But they are laborers or people milling around near their homes or apartment buildings. Or, they're poor. You, on the other hand, are not a laborer and most likely not poor by Thai standards. Short pants are considered impolite.

Next, remember to dress up a bit. Why wear T-shirts everywhere you travel? Meet your Thai sweetheart with a collared shirt or a buttoned shirt. I'm not saying you must come to a date or go to the grocery store in a suit and tie, but neither do you have the freedom to walk around in flip flops, cut-off sweatpants, and your favorite faded T-shirt. Well, you

do have the freedom in a legal sense, and you do have the freedom to ignore my advice, but you will lose respect in public. If that is something you do not worry about, then make sure you find a Thai woman who is equally uninterested in how people view you in public. However, if your Thai woman does not care about this, then you might have lowered your standards a bit too much.

Khun Toon wants men to understand that there is a difference in the way you dress within your neighborhood and, say, at least two kilometers outside your neighborhood. This advice is for couples living in Thailand. Though the Land of Smiles is very hot, Thais do not wear short pants in public. Yes, you will find Thais in shorts, but Toon guarantees that the person is within close proximity of home, if they're not at the beach. Short pants are still considered impolite and if you strut around Bangkok, or any major town in the provinces, you will be looked at unfavorably.

Her family and other scary things

Money can't buy happiness, but it can sure buy peace

14

Nosy relatives

In this chapter, I will discuss your in-laws. You might have concluded from earlier chapters that when you marry a Thai, you marry her family. So when you choose a woman to court, take a good look at her family too because you will be their future loan officer, one that never gets interest and almost never recoups his money.

As I explained earlier, and it's worth repeating, a Thai woman will increase her self-esteem by helping her family increase their living standards. If you take this away from your bride, she will lose her self-worth. If you refuse to help her show generosity to her family, you will strip away her identity. I've heard the expression, "Give me liberty or give me death." For a Thai, it would be something like, "Let me be generous or let me die." Just as a Western man values his independence, so a Thai woman values her ability to be generous.

However, you'll find times when your wife is pressured to show generosity rather than giving out of her own free will. A very typical exchange between your wife and an in-law may go like this.

"I need 2,000 baht."

Your wife will say, "I don't have it."

The relative will have a simple solution: "Just get it from your *farang* husband."

You can imagine what happens next. Every time she asks for money, you will think it's for family. You begin not to trust her and feel that her family is insincere and only calls her when they're in need. This will develop into one-sided, light-hearted banter when you join her in visiting her family. Don't be surprised to hear, "Hey, Bob. I don't have a car. Do you think you can buy me one?" or "Bob, my motorcycle broke down. A new one costs 10,000 baht. Can you transfer the money to me?" They'll laugh after they say it to help relieve you of the shock of their request, but you still feel there is something behind the joke. A hint, perhaps? While some relatives will stop there, others will repeat their requests and expect a response, not just a smile. It may come off as a joke, but they would happily accept a gift if you happen to misunderstand and think they are serious.

Since isolating your wife from her family is out of the question, and you can't change the fact that you have fallen in love with a woman whose family is numerous and poor, you'll need some help on how to deal with the relatives and still keep your wallet from developing a hole.

To deal with this sticky situation, the first thing you can do is set a budget each month for her family. By family, I mean her parents and any younger siblings that she is responsible for. Determine this amount before you get married. Make it as clear as possible to your soon-to-be-bride how much you can set aside each month for her to give, and don't fluctuate. Make sure she passes this information on to her family too because by the second month there might be a request to increase the amount. Stand firm and remind her that this was the amount the two of you agreed upon before you got married. She will be on your side,

but she needs the authority of your words to pass on to her younger sister who thought she could spend her amount dancing at a nightclub and expect you to recoup her losses. Stand firm and her family will understand that this is the amount you will give regularly and they'll have to manage monthly with that amount.

Always transfer or hand the money to her relatives on time. If you're late, it will be seen as a slight against them. Treat this like any other bill that has a due date: pay the full amount and pay it on time. Stressful relations is the interest that comes with late payments.

The distant relatives will show up eventually, too. Suppose you've solved the money situation with your wife's parents and maybe her younger siblings that she's responsible for. But you haven't accounted for the cousins, second cousins, friends of neighbors of your wife's third cousin's ex-husband who have heard of their distant relative's *farang* husband and want their share of the pie. You will likely have these people – who didn't come to your wedding or send not even a congratulations card – call your wife and ask for a handout. Thais live to show generosity, but even we get annoyed by some requests. Yet, we'll see what we can do to help before rejecting them.

It would make your wife's heart glad to help any relative in need, immediate or distant. Try scraping together a few hundred or thousand baht here and there to send. Don't take out a loan or give more than you can. If you can only give an amount that's less than what they asked for, send it anyway.

If it's a relative that your wife is not close to and the amount is too inconvenient, you can stand firm and say no. Read your wife. Does she seem annoyed by the request too? Does she seem to want you to help her say 'no'? Quite often you might have to be the bad guy. I mean your wife will have to decline the request and put the blame on you, even though she is in complete agreement with you. Allowing her to use the stereotype of the stingy foreigner helps her save face. She'll appreciate your support in this matter and for willingly being the scapegoat and will find a way to make it up to you later with love and devotion. And maybe lots of sex!

Depending on the size of her family, these annoying money-grubbing requests may never stop, but by working together and understanding each other (her needs and your limitations), her family will respect that you two are united and stand firm when you need to and are generous when you can be.

15

Visiting your in-laws

Hopefully by this point you have realized how important family is to a Thai woman. If something about her family bothers you, the worst thing you could do is try to separate your wife from her family and make two camps: You and your wife versus her family. You will fail. Your Thai wife will not let you do this. She has a duty to support her family and at times you will feel that you are second to them, especially to her parents and younger siblings.

There is no way to get around this. Pardon me for repeating it, but it's something you have to accept if you want to marry a Thai woman. Even if you marry someone whose parents have passed away and who doesn't have any siblings, she will try to find someone to fill that role of the dependent elder. The best way to deal with this is to have the right attitude.

The right attitude is not showing resentment for her family's position in your wife's heart. They will sense your attitude when you are on their territory: their home. How you act when visiting your wife's family is crucial for the peace between you and your wife. They will watch you carefully and discuss your attitude with your wife, so don't embarrass her.

Even if you can't speak Thai, try communicating. Communicating involves more than using words. Try smiling and asking your wife to translate your interest in things you see around the house or village. Show your in-laws that you are interested in knowing them and their life, especially if you are visiting a village or small town which is very likely.

You might marry a smartly-dressed office girl, but when you visit her family in Isaan you find a dirty, untidy, dusty home surrounded by fields and wild animals. You may also find that her parents wear simple,

traditional clothes that you would have thrown away years ago if they were yours. Life in the countryside is very different to Bangkok, but you must not stick your nose up at your wife's family. If you do, your wife will be hurt because deep down this is still her home. No matter how long she may have been working in Bangkok, she will still be proud of her province, no matter how backward it may seem to you. Looking down on her family means you are looking down on her, too.

Your wife also carries some responsibility for helping you fit in with her family. If she is not doing her part, then you do have the right to bring this up with her and explain your feelings. Your wife should not ignore you and leave you sitting in front of the small television set watching a Thai comedy show – this is a standard form of torture not sanctioned by the U.N.

Instead, she should tell funny and interesting stories about you to her parents so they get to know your personality and values. She should willingly be the middle person and do her best to help bridge the cultural and linguistic gap between you and her parents. Her responsibility is no more than yours and definitely no less. Before tying the knot, it would be good to see how she handles her role as the mediator when she brings you to visit her family. Make sure your bride-to-be is pulling her weight too.

If you find it difficult to get yourself involved with her family and you find yourself just sitting and not speaking, but not wanting to appear bored, wait for your wife to say something. She may ask if you are okay (not because she noticed, most likely because someone else noticed and brought it to her attention). Take that opportunity to ask her for her help. Tell her to translate something you want to say. Get her involved. Hopefully she will catch on and realize she needs to do her part too. The Western way is to make this clear before arriving at her parents' home, but planning ahead is not a skill that has evolved in Thai society. Your wife will have to see how uncomfortable you are during the visit and hear your plea for help, and put the two together to understand her role.

16

Raising kids: Acting like monkeys and giving them names

Hardly a visit will go by without relatives and friends asking you and your wife when the two of you plan to have children. The childless couple is rare in Thailand. Unless there is a medical condition, Thai couples are expected to multiply. If you are the rare reader who does not plan on having children, then you can keep answering this nosy question with: "In the near future." If you do plan on having them, this chapter is for you!

I remember one day when I went to visit a Thai friend. Her husband is American and they have one son, about four years old. I was helping around the house, spending time with my friend and also watching the boy. At one point, like all boys do, he started acting up and acting crazy. I asked him, "Do you want to act like a monkey?" He said, "Yeah, a monkey!" And he started making monkey noises and hopping around with his elbows bent and hands under his armpits. I was dumbfounded. What went wrong? If this were a Thai kid, he would have behaved immediately because no Thai kid wants to be seen as an animal.

This story just illustrates the little differences between cultures. And there are many differences. It is hard to put them into one book; you'll just have to experience most of them for yourself and learn how to discern them. Most books rehash the basics: Don't touch a Thai person's head, don't point with your foot, and so on. But most educated Westerners don't do those things in front of strangers in their own countries anyway!

I learned that day that Western kids like to make animal sounds and act like animals. So I could not discipline him in that way. I just let it go because it wasn't my place to discipline him, but even if it were, I'm not sure what I should have done. Maybe do it the American way and take a belt and whip him and tell him how it hurts me more?

Deciding how to raise your children will be the biggest challenge of your marriage. Should they be Thai? Should they be Western? Since they are mixed, raise them to be both? The answer to these questions really depends on where you will live. If you live in Thailand, they'll have to learn to fit in. If in the West, it is the same.

I have some false beliefs I want to dispel. Many parents believe it confuses children to learn more than one language. This is completely wrong. It is nothing more than an advantage for a child to be fluent in more than one language.

Let me tell you a joke. What do you call a person who speaks three languages? Trilingual. What do you call a person who speaks two languages? Bilingual. What do you call a person who speaks one language? American.

The point is that most people in the world speak more than one language and do so fluently. There is no evidence, except anecdotes from uninformed parents, that speaking more than one language is harmful for children. Being able to use a second language can open so many doors: more job opportunities, access to all the literature and culture of the people who use that language, and so on. Certainly there is a time when children have to learn to separate the use of the two or more languages, but they do so successfully.

Another misguided belief is that bilingualism means using two languages equally. Actually, most bilingual people do not use both languages in the same context. In their lives, the place and time for each language is definite. A Malaysian Chinese child may learn to use Hakka within the home, Mandarin when speaking with the Chinese community outside the home, then Bahasa for government and educational contexts, and English for business and religious services. Each context would have its own level of formality. The average Christian Chinese child would not need to know religious terms in Malay, but the Muslim child would. A Chinese would not need to use colloquial English with the grandparents, as he or she would be required to learn honorific terms in one or more Chinese dialects. So we can say the child is multilingual, but in no way is the child expected to be able to use each language *equally* well in all contexts.

I say this to explain that bilingual education is sometimes not natural. Bilingual schools force students to use two languages equally, but in the real world that is rarely the case. So don't worry about finding the right bilingual school and then giving up on raising your child to speak both English (or French, German, Swedish) and Thai because you think they lack the right school support. You can be their support at home. Have them at least learn to speak Thai in the home and English at school. If the father's native language is not English, have your child learn three languages! The father speaks his language to the child, the Thai mother speaks hers, and both of you support their learning of English both at home and at school (I'm assuming that you and your Thai wife will speak English together). Forget about confusing your child. It is natural for children to learn when and where they are to use each language. They will grow up having more advantages in many areas of life, from cultural to professional. The world needs more people with wider world views.

After you have the language issue settled, let's discuss the cultural differences between the West and Thailand when it comes to naming your children. One day my husband joked that he wanted to have two daughters and they would be named after our mothers. At first I was a bit offended that he would mock my mother.

"How did I mock her?" he asked.

"Because she's not dead yet!" I said.

In Thai culture, we do not name a child after a living relative. You have to wait until he or she has died. Then the name can be used again. In the West, naming a child after a living relative is a normal practice. But in Thailand, we do not have such titles as "junior." You can pick a name that is similar to the elder relative's name, but it cannot be the very same.

Conclusion

I hope you have had a few laughs while reading this book and that you are even more determined to make your marriage with your Thai sweetheart a success. Deep down all women are the same and have the same needs, but culture determines how those needs are met. So, don't be intimidated by cultural differences. Understand the reason behind a Thai person's actions, and you'll find that you have the same needs as the Thai. The two of you are only going about fulfilling those needs in different ways. Of course, choosing the right Thai woman for you will help smooth the road bumps that you will inevitably hit. Keep the right attitude and you'll learn to live with a Thai woman, and survive!

Patcharaporn 'Pop' Soisangwan was born and raised in Thailand. She majored in English at Chiang Mai University and now lives and studies in Ashland, Ohio.